Contents

FRONT ENDPAPERS: A pair of color canaries and their nestlings. Photo by Harry V. Lacey.
BACK ENDPAPERS: Yorkshire canary, a type variety. Photo by Harry V. Lacey.

COVER: A domestic canary enjoying fresh greenfood.

TITLE PAGE: Young rollers bred in England. Photo by H.V. Lacey.

Originally published in German by Franckh'sche Verlagshandlung, W. Keller. & Co., Stuttgart/1976 under the name *Kamersanger im Federkleid: Kanarienvogel.* First edition © 1976 by Franckh'sche Verlagshandlung. © 1981 by T.F.H. Publications, Inc. Ltd. for English translation. A considerable amount of additional new material has been added to the literal German-English translation, including but not limited to additional photographs. Copyright is also claimed for this new material.

ISBN 0-87666-875-9

© 1981 by T.F.H. Publications, Inc. Ltd.

Distributed in the U.S. by T.F.H. Publications, Inc., 211 West Sylvania Avenue, PO Box 427, Neptune, NJ 07753; in England by T.F.H. (Gt. Britain) Ltd., 13 Nutley Lane, Reigate, Surrey; in Canada to the pet trade by Rolf C. Hagen Ltd., 3225 Sartelon Street, Montreal 382, Quebec; in Canada to the book trade by H & L Pet Supplies, Inc., 27 Kingston Crescent, Kitchener, Ontario N28 2T6; in Southeast Asia by Y.W. Ong, 9 Lorong 36 Geylang, Singapore 14; in Australia and the South Pacific by Pet Imports Pty. Ltd., P.O. Box 149, Brookvale 2100, N.S.W. Australia; in South Africa by Valid Agencies, P.O. Box 51901, Randburg 2125 South Africa. Published by T.F.H. Publications, Inc., Ltd., the British Crown Colony of Hong Kong.

SINGING CANARIES

Klaus Speicher

Left: The angular and high shoulders of this Belgian canary may appear abnormal to someone who is not familiar with the breed. A Vogelpark Walsrode photo.
Below: Shown here are just a few of the many colored varieties of canaries bred today.

Preface

In a variety of ways, people alive today are dependent on machines and automation, for without these our modern life would be unthinkable. Indeed, an increasingly greater part of our daily routine is being regulated by technical equipment.

However, we human beings need Nature, because of our origin and because of the way we are made. The more technology takes over and the smaller the natural reaches of plant and animal kingdom become, the more we are driven to keep in touch with Nature in our own homes. Where once domestic pets were daily companions of man, small indoor animals have increasingly taken their place. Among them, birds occupy a privileged position. It is only now that we are able to see animals as they really are and that people have come to accept the fact that an

animal's behavior cannot be measured by our own. For centuries man misinterpreted the reasons behind animal behavior because he humanized them. Since then, however, man's relationship to the animal has undergone a fundamental change. This has, of course, also rubbed off on bird keeping and bird breeding as a hobby. And canaries, which have been popular from days of old, are no exception. In spite of the obvious fact that these birds have become the cultivated creations of the art of breeding, their nature and their living requirements can only be understood by us if we use our intelligence a little and see the whole bird, that is, their natural origin together with the new man-and-animal relationship. To try and get this across and to talk to the bird fancier about the requirements of the feathered friends he has chosen to share his home with are the purposes of this work. The contemplative joys of genuine nature-watching can be found even in the contact with a mere canary. May this volume, therefore, help to ensure that in the future too as many nature-lovers as possible will take canaries into their own homes in order to enjoy them.

1

1. It is possible to teach your pet to perform "tricks." This canary has learned that the white drawer, and not the black, contains seeds. Photo by A. Barry. **2.** Keepers of any kind of canary must see to it that the cage (breeding cage especially) is clean. Photo by H.V. Lacey.

Left: Unlike the wild canary, which is restricted to the Atlantic islands, the serin *(Serinus serinus)* is widely distributed in Europe. A Vogelpark Walsrode photo. *Right, below:* As a result of selection and cross-breeding, many breeds of domestic canaries no longer resemble the color or shape of the wild canary. Photo by H.V. Lacey.

History of Canaries

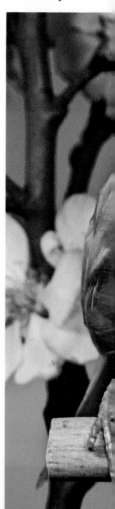

Like all domestic animals, the canary too—in its many different forms and breeds—is descended from a free-living wild form. The wild canary, or to use its scientific name, *Serinus c. canaria,* is a small finch native to the Canary Islands. These Atlantic islands, which today have become a favorite holiday resort for Europeans, have long been known as the Happy Islands on account of their perpetual spring-like weather. The wild canary also inhabits the Azores and Madeira. The first detailed description of this bird in its natural habitat was provided by K. Bolle after a journey in 1858. This was quite late, considering that canaries had already been adopted by man since the second half of the 15th century. The modern tourist can no longer imagine the hardship, exertion, and adventures involved in those voyages of discovery that

were made in past epochs, long before airplanes or even steamships existed. Alexander von Humboldt, on his journey to South America, also visited the Canary Islands and he too described the "Canary birds."

In appearance the wild form resembles our contemporary green canaries so widely kept everywhere, except that it is of a more slender or, if one feels inclined to say, more elegant build. Its habits are very similar to those of the serin (*Serinus serinus*), to whom it is closely related. At one time the two birds were actually thought to be two regional variations of one and the same species. This theory collapsed when more about the history of the canary became known. The two birds are without a doubt two distinctly separate species. Open parkland, fruit farms, slopes with not much vegetation—these are the habitats of the canary. In February or, most commonly, at the beginning of March nest-building begins. The bird is also found in the gardens of villages and smaller towns, and here the species starts to breed particularly early. The bird is a tree-dweller, rather like the chaffinch. Its nest-building technique also resembles that of the chaffinch, except that the nest is located nearer the outer end of the branches, similar to that of the European goldfinch. Males and females differ in the color of their plumage. The difference is only slight, however. The male is deep-green, with yellow markings on the head (frontal stripe, margin round the eye, and cheeks); rump and upper tail coverts are of a pure yellowish-green. The female is altogether more grayish in color, and the green only appears in a few areas (eye-stripe, shoulders, rump, and less brightly on the chest). In older males the yellow in the plumage looks more intense than in the young birds. Breeding proceeds in very much the same way as in other members of the finch family. The female incubates the eggs and both parents take part in the rearing of the young. The birds are particularly partial to half-ripe seeds (milk stage) and all sorts of greenfood. This is an important point to remember for anyone wishing to keep canaries; greenfood must be on the menu at all times.

In its natural environment the canary feeds on a wide range of seeding plants containing starch and oil: among them, above all, the seeds of the crucifers and compositae, notably cabbage, lettuce, groundsel, and sow-thistle varieties, as well as the seeds of chickweed, plantain, mercury and poppy. A particular favorite of the canaries are the seeds of the so-called canary grass (*Phalaris canariensis*), which under the name "canary seed" still remain an important component of every available canary food. Wild canaries further take the seeds of certain millet varieties, as well as picking out the seeding heads of sugar cane. The latter activity earned them the name "little sugar birds," under which they continued to be sold for a long time after their importation into Spain. Outside the breeding season the canaries congregate into numerous flocks—and these flocks roam about, just like the European goldfinches, for example, in late summer and in the fall.

Today such wild canaries offered on the bird market are few and far between. Frequently, the birds that are being sold as wild canaries are yellow canaries (*Crithagra flaviventris*) or Cape canaries (*Serinus canicollis*), two species which occur on the African mainland. The "South American canaries" or "Pampas canaries" that have recently come into the market are members of the species *Sycalis flaveola* (saffron finch); they are in no way related to the canary.

Anyone wishing to buy wild specimens would do well to seek the advice of an experienced ornithologist if he wants to be sure that the birds offered are genuine canaries.

In the care of a hobbyist, wild canaries, as compared to domesticated birds of whatever breed, tend to be problem pets, and only the experienced breeder should have a go at them. Plenty of greenstuff and half-ripe and germinated seeds are absolutely essential if the birds are to survive for any length of time.

DOMESTIC CANARIES

Although the group of islands west of Africa was already known to the Romans and had, in fact, been named *Canarias* by them (because of the many big dogs occurring there—*canis* being the Latin for dog), the conquest was reserved for the Spanish. The first of the Spanish invasions took place in 1473 and the final one in 1496. And very soon after the Spanish had established themselves on the islands the seamen developed a liking for those little green birds which so quickly grew tame in the cage. Furthermore, these birds sang beautifully. Soldiers and sailors therefore brought their small feathered singers back home to their native country with them, either to enjoy them in their leisure hours or to honor their lady love with this curious and rare "souvenir." The "little sugar birds," as they were frequently called, became so fashionable that it was soon a matter of etiquette for every suitor to present such a bird to his lady. The aristocracy had increasingly valuable golden cages made for this purpose. The mariners soon realized they were on to a good thing with these little songsters; business flourished, and they brought back more and more of the birds. In the Cadiz area (a small port) a little trade center for canaries evolved. The males were particularly sought after; they alone are capable of such beautiful song.

An escalating demand, and the far from regular journeys of the ships in those days, prompted the question as to how these popular birds

1

1. The bright red male of the hooded siskin *(Spinus cucullatus)* is utilized by breeders in the production of red-colored canaries. A Vogelpark Walsrode photo. 2. In this dimorphic red factor female canary the bright red color is limited to the face, bend of the wing and the rump. 3. A red factor male canary.

2

might be obtained more quickly and securely. In the cloisters the monks tried to breed the canaries in their care; and, lo and behold, it was not all that difficult.

This, then, is where the history of the canary as a pet began. Behind medieval cloister walls the destiny of a species of bird, which was to become the companion of man like no other before it, was decided. When the Renaissance was at its zenith in Europe, chance and luck helped to create this domestic animal.

There are a number of finches which are easier to breed in captivity: bullfinch, greenfinch, siskin, goldfinch. All these birds reproduce much more readily in cage and aviary than the little green canary. It must be considered pure chance, therefore, that serious and successful breeding attempts were made with just this problem bird. But a lot of luck comes into it as well, for these breeding experiments were begun in southern Spain, in the Mediterranean climate. There is no doubt that the similarity between this climate and that of the canary's native habitat was responsible for tipping the scales in favor of success. In a more northerly part of Europe these breeding attempts would almost certainly have failed. With each successive generation the birds bred more readily and more successfully. Their popularity increased so rapidly that they were already described, albeit very sketchily, by the grand master of zoology Conrad Gesner (1516-1565) in his *Natural History of Birds*. He gave them the name *Canaria avicula*. The reference in an Italian book by Aldrovandi of 1610, a general work on ornithology, already contains details. Thus, the livelier yellow coloration of the male is emphasized and grass seeds (*Phalaris canariensis*) are mentioned as the canaries' favorite food.

Italy was the center of intellectual Europe in those days of late Renaissance and early Baroque. And inevitably our canary, too, travelled from Spain to Italy. In many pictures of that period we can see the lady of the house portrayed with her little feathered darling. What makes these pictures even more interesting with regard to the history of the canary is their documentation of the first change shown by the canary while undergoing domestication.

The uniformly greenish-brown color of its plumage is interrupted by lighter, yellow, patches; the bird is now mottled. This partial absence of dark pigments (melanin pigments) occurs in all domesticated animals. With this the racial history of the canaries has begun. It is still continuing and will not end while these animals continue to be bred. All living creatures are subject to constant change. This variability of animals found in nature is exploited by man—that is, adapted by him to fit in with his goals—when he breeds animals of whatever kind.

16

The Spaniards made very sure that no female canaries were exported. Thus they secured a monopoly of the canary trade for themselves, which they managed to preserve for nearly a hundred years. By that time Italy, too, had canary breeders, and from Italy the canary culture continued to spread.

THE TYROL AND THE HARZ MOUNTAINS

Canary-breeding in Italy spread from south to north into the Alpine valleys. As early as 1622 Olina supplied a tolerably good description (with a drawing) of the canary and paid tribute to its singing talent.

An old myth crept into the literature on canaries which was stubbornly adopted by many authors and still crops up today. According to this tale, a ship carrying canaries as part of its cargo was caught in a storm on its way from the Canary Islands to Spain. The ship eventually ran aground off the island of Elba, and the canaries escaped onto the island. There they mated with the native finches and reproduced. In the light of our present knowledge of ornithology and animal-breeding, this theory that has come down to us does not hold water and must be banished into the realm of fiction.

There is no basis, no evidence, for the assumption that other wild finch species besides *Serinus canaria* were involved in the domestication of the canary (with the much later exception of the hooded siskin, *Spinus cucullatus,* for color-bred birds). No interchange of genes between species took place. The changes that became the basis for a development of different races were purely the result of mutation. One fact, however, undoubtedly encouraged the idea that crossbreeding had taken place in those early days: the population of serins *(Serinus serinus)* found on the island of Elba have a plumage much more conspicuous in color than those on the continent. In those days, however, the range of the serin did not extend to Central Europe. The serin originally came from the Atlas countries in northern Africa and for the past 200 years has been spreading steadily northwards. It is possible that the serins on Elba with their bright color led people to believe that these birds had crossbred with the wild canary. Whether the Italians ever caught these birds and brought them to the market as "canaries" is equally unproved and unlikely.

What is certain, however, is that the canary trade was not conducted on a really big scale until it took root in the Tyrol. When mining decreased, the Tyrolese mountain population turned to canary breeding as a means of earning their livelihood. Although canary breeding in the Tyrol already began at the end of the 17th century, it did not have its boom time until the 18th century. The popular operetta *Der*

1. Gloster canaries are small birds (ideally, not more than 4 ¾ inches long). They are bred with or without a crest. The crest consists of a group of feathers radiating from a common center on top of the head. 2. A new color recessive white canary. This breed is distinct from the dominant white in its heredity and appearance. 3. A male Gloster fancy canary which was known to have produced black young earlier was utilized in the breeding of this sooty-black bird. Photos by H.V. Lacey.

Vogelhandler (The Bird Dealer) is about that period. Every year, late in the summer, the dealers set off. It was a great day for the poor mountain-dwellers and, accordingly, turned into a festive occasion. The men were escorted outside the boundaries of the town. On their backs they carried the "bird baskets," containers especially made for the purpose of holding small cages for 200 birds. In this way the Tyrolese bird-dealers brought the canary to all countries in Europe. Particularly the big trading cities were visited at regular intervals. The bird-dealers journeyed as far as Russia, Turkey, Egypt, and England to find customers for their feathered merchandise.

As early as the last quarter of the 18th century there existed in Imst, a small town in the northern Tyrol, a society that every year, after the breeding season had ended, sent buyers to the canary-breeders in Germany and Switzerland to purchase the young.

When industrialization changed the lonely wooded Harz mountains into a busy mining center in the 19th century, the contractors also hired the Tyrolese highlanders to go down into the dark shafts, as there was a general shortage of labor. The Tyrolese came and brought their canaries with them. Here in the Harz Mountains these simple high-landers were destined to create what undoubtedly became the most famous canary breed of all: the German Roller (*Harzer Edelroller*). Up to then breeding had been more or less haphazard; no attention was paid to song. But once the various breeders in the Harz Mountains started to build up their own stock, matters became rather different. What they did was not a goal-directed creation of breeding stock—there was no detailed breeding program. After all, at that time the laws of heredity and genetics and the principles which apply to mating were quite unknown. To a greater or lesser degree, however, each breeder bred along particular "lines." Annually, at the beginning of fall, the big dealers sent their "taggers" to all the breeders in the small towns and villages of the Harz Mountains. These were the buyers, but they were also the first experts on canary song. They already sorted the young males into various classes fetching different prices. Birds which had a pleasant, pure voice and sang pleasing "tours" fetched a higher price than those that produced a loud noise with the beak open that were not so pleasant to listen to. Consequently, the breeders tried to produce as many of the good birds as possible in order to make bigger profits. To improve their stock they held on to those males that delivered valuable tours. The tagger was also expected to be able to sex the animals. After all, he did not always have the time to listen to the song of every bird he was buying. To be on the safe side, it was therefore necessary for him to be familiar with the visual distinguishing characteristics as well. From the sixties of the previous century onward we can say that a true *Edelroller* culture existed in Germany. That the taggers did a lot to get it going there can be little doubt. They were, in effect, the forerunners of today's judges. Shortly after 1870 the first canary breeders' associations were formed. To start with they were just sub-groups of the existing poultry-farming societies. By this time canary breeding was no longer confined to the few areas where it was practiced on a large scale as a means of earning a livelihood. In the cities, and increasingly in smaller townships and in the country as well, canary breeding became a popular hobby with bird fanciers. Improved transport connections, industrial development, and not least the information media led to an unexpected increase in support. A magazine devoted exclusively to canaries became the most important connecting link between breeders and hobbyist and dealers.

The names Seifert, Trute, and Erntges will remain synonymous with the creation of the *Edelroller*. Among the countless birds bred in the Harz Mountains their stocks were the first to include individuals noted for their special qualities. From these birds, thanks to a lot of hard work by the breeders, the purebred Rollers of today originated. In the Harz Mountains the breeding of canaries, as far as the practical work is concerned, was done mainly by women. While the man followed his occupation, a working day then was 12 hours, the woman saw to the birds. Invariably, the birds were propagated in "bird rooms," that is, inside a large flight males and females could choose their own mates and go about their breeding business without human intervention. This type of bird culture has now ceased to be employed not only because of the many disturbances but also, and particularly, because of the uncontrolled parentage of the young. Where pure breeds are desired this method is not permissible anyway. Nowadays one rarely comes across a breeder who is concerned purely with propagating his canaries without paying attention to special racial characteristics.

The *Deutscher Kanarienzuchter-Bund (DKB) e.V.* (German canary breeders' association) with over 10,000 members now sets the standards. It belongs to the international breeders' organization, the *Confederation Ornithologique Mondiale (COM)*, which includes more than thirty countries from all over the world. Everywhere in the world song canaries are now judged and given points according to a universally agreed-on scale that was devised in Germany and which serves as a useful guideline for breeders, judges, and hobbyists.

WORLDWIDE CANARY TRADE

Today canaries are transported everywhere in the world. The little

1. A family of roller canaries. As rollers are bred for their song, appearance is not particularly important. Photo by H.V. Lacey. 2. A border canary with heavily variegated plumage. A Vogelpark Walsrode photo. 3. A clear yellow border canary should not have any dark color in its plumage. A Vogelpark Walsrode photo. 4. Another pair of border canaries: a self green and a variegated yellow. Photo by H.V. Lacey.

feathered chamber singer of the bird world, our canary, has long since become cosmopolitan. In all countries of the world, on every continent, it has its flock of supporters, and organized breeders' associations have sprung up everywhere. They arrange contests to establish who has produced the most handsome specimen of a breed and whose songsters deliver the best tours. The canary's increasing popularity is directly linked to the development of universal means of transport and communication.

In the Middle Ages the sailing ships of the glorious Spanish fleet brought the first green canaries from their native islands to southern Europe. For a long time sailing ships remained the sole means of transport by which canaries reached the major coastal trading centers of that time.

The Tyrolese bird traders made their journeys to as far as Constantinople, St. Petersburg, Paris, and Antwerp, on foot along the highways. It took them weeks to get from one city to another, and they were away from home for months at a time.

With the advent of the railway the birds reached their destination much more quickly—it now only took a few days to dispatch them from one place in Europe to another. This was a decisive factor in the founding of breeders' societies. Only now could shows and contests become practical. That such a delicate cargo consisting of living canaries requires expert packaging and care if it is not to come to any harm goes without saying.

The steamships, however, made the jump across the oceans possible. The greatest export trade of canaries to all parts of the world developed in Germany. Ruhe and Reiche are the most famous names among the exporters of that time. The big steamships of the overseas lines had specially designed bird cabins rented out permanently to canary exporters for their birds.

To give the reader an idea of the dimensions of the business I shall quote a few figures. Between July 1882 and April 1883 alone, at least 120,000 canaries travelled to New York from the Reiche firm in Alfeld. Over and above that, Mr. Reiche dispatched 10,500 male canaries to South America, 5,600 to Australia and 3,000 to South Africa. In addition, about 30,000 specimens went to other European countries (France, Belgium, England, Russia, and Austria) while about 12,000 found takers in Germany. The number of canary males bred in the Harz town of Andreasberg alone is estimated at up to 40,000 annually. Prices paid by the wholesale company buyers ranged from DM 2.50 to 4.00 per bird, depending on the quality of the song.

In the 19th century the domestic trade in the previous century was conducted mainly by travelling salesmen who went to the bigger German cities with their "better wares" and to the smaller townships and villages with specimens of "lower" quality. The latter more often than not included females which the salesmen tried to sell off as males.

The really big breeding businesses have ceased to exist. Nevertheless, the Harz Mountains have remained the seat of a few canary exporters. These continue, even today, to supply particularly American customers (with some romantic streak in them) who feel they need to possess the "genuine" Harz Roller. By means of advertisements in bird magazines the Harz Mountain exporters collect export canaries from all over Germany. Then today's big jumbo jets carry their feathered cargo to all the different continents at the greatest possible speed. To Rio de Janeiro the flight from Frankfurt/Main takes roughly 11 hours, to Toronto in Canada ten hours, to New York seven to eight hours. Even the most distant town on the globe can be reached within as little as three days. The implications for the bird trade are self-evident. Wherever people travel, birds travel as well, to give pleasure to some hobbyist. Canary cargoes are carried by the airlines the whole year 'round.

The airport authorities are only too pleased to find favorable flight-connections for birds, as not every type of plane is suitable; some do not have an air-conditioned cabin. In the normal freight room the temperature can drop to minus 30° C and more, depending on altitude. For the safe and speedy dispatch of canaries from Germany to the neighboring countries today's railway service is excellently suited. Again, every station is only too willing to give information and advice and to help with the selecting of fast and reliable train connections. For the breeder who belongs to an association and takes part in shows it has become standard practice to send his birds by rail or plane, depending on the distance between his home town and the place of exhibition.

Left: In the early days of song canary culture the nightingale, a bird well known for its song, was utilized to "teach" young canaries to sing like itself. *Below:* A singing canary, a roller, in the nest. Photo by H.V. Lacey.

The Canary Song

Anyone stepping inside a pet shop nowadays and taking a look at the cages with canaries will be astonished at the great variety of colors confronting him. There are red and gray, green and isabel, silver-colored and white, pink and yellow birds, and pied ones in addition. At some distance from these there will usually also be a few tiny little cages, each containing only a single bird, and these will be described as genuine song canaries. To the question as to what the difference is, the reply tends to be: "Those are color birds, but they do not sing, and the others, in the small cages, are real song canaries—only they can sing."

Many of the older breeders specializing in song canaries will say something like that, too. They do not think much of the modern interest in breeding for color. Of course all male canaries sing no matter

what variety they belong to. Male color canaries also sing their own song, but their song is not as intricately structured as that of a Harz Mountain Roller. The latter has, after all, been subject to special selective breeding for generations, with the breeding birds selected solely for the quality of their song. Conversely, breeders interested in color have always devoted their efforts to beauty of appearance, almost to the exclusion of everything else. Song was not taken into consideration. For this reason the voice of a color bird is less cultivated, and its song is loud and on the shrill side, full of high-pitched notes which are almost painful to the listener's ear. A layman who wants to learn something about canary song will certainly not learn anything, when he visits a show or contest, merely by listening to experienced Roller breeders discussing this topic among themsleves. Here he hears about "heavy hollow bell" (*Schwere Hohlklingel*), "dragging hollow" (*Schleppendem Hohl*), about "flat flutes" (*Flachen Pfeifen*), and watery bell (*Waessriger Klingel*). He hears terms like "four flutes" (*Vierer-Pfeifen*), "six hollow" (*Sechser-Hohl*) and "seven bass" (*Siebener-Knorre*). Nevertheless, anyone who is a little bit musical can acquire a certain amount of knowledge about canary song simply by listening to the birds themselves.

THE ROLLER (EDELROLLER)

This may be considered the fundamental rule: everything that is delivered with a closed beak is worth having. What the bird sings with an open beak is of inferior quality. This applies to the song of the *Edelroller* as it is mainly bred in Germany.

Nomenclature has been the subject of disagreement in very recent times. Many breeders insist that only the term "song canary" is appropriate. This is, however, misleading in that there are other varieties of song canary, such as the Belgian Waterslager, to name only one. The name "Harz Roller" for the German song canary is no longer quite correct either, as these birds have long since ceased to be bred solely in the Harz Mountains. Furthermore, today's Harz Roller is a much improved version of that from the previous century. The modern hollow-bass-flute stocks have left the early Harz Mountain bird far behind in quality as regards richness and depth of tone of the basic tours. I, therefore, hold that only the name *Edelroller* is suitable for the modern Roller canary. This canary has long been bred in other countries as well, although the German stocks continue to be in the lead with regard to quality. Tradition is clearly of advantage here. Some breeding stocks in Germany have been in one and the same family for generations. The grandfather had bred Edelrollers and then the father, and now the son.

Annually, in the fall, all the canary-breeding societies in Germany hold their competitions. The best birds are sent to the regional contests of the different societies, where they compete against birds from other societies and are judged for the quality of their song. The judges for song canaries are experts with years of experience who break down a bird's song into clearly defined passages (known as *"tours"*) in order to examine them for their musical quality. Precisely 30 minutes are allowed. In this time the birds have to go through their repertoire. They are specially trained for this. After their cages are darkened for a time, when the light returns the birds deliver their song. This is an oversimplification, however; in reality it takes a great deal of skill and expertise on the part of the breeder to teach the young males to become master singers.

The song of the modern *Edelroller* canary is characterized by four basic, or main, tours.

(1) The *hollow roll (Hohlrolle)* if delivered perfectly, is intensified into pure vocalization. It sounds something like this: *hohohoho* or *hoohoohoohoo* or *houhouhouhouhou*. It is a clearly defined tour in the song of a Roller and characteristic of the *Edelroller* variety. No other breed brings such tonal depth and such melting softness into the voice as a hollow-roller does when he masters this tour.

(2) *Knorre* is the German term for the *bass-roll* tour in the canary's song. This passage sounds as it is spelt. The consonant *r* must clearly dominate this delivery of the bird's song, roughly like this: *rororororororo* or *rorrr*. The vowel *oe* (as *hoe* in English) is not always woven into the song very distinctly, but delivery must always be sonorous and voluminous so that the bass character of the *Knorre* is fully brought out.

(3) *Flutes (Pfeifen)* is a clearly defined tour which is not delivered in a "rolling" form (as are the two preceding ones, for example). But the canary has two separate, very different, flutes. One is a kind of call-note, used for communication. This, as a rule, is the first sound the bird makes when it wakes up in the morning. The male song canaries in their small training cages also start to "communicate" by means of this call-flute when they are taken out of the dusky darkness of their training quarters and placed on the table in groups of four to practice their songs. On the other hand, flutes as basic tours are different: the bird blows or breathes them out in clearly defined bars. They are particularly desirable at a low pitch. It sounds something like this: *doo-doo-doo* or *dow-dow-dow* or *diu-diu-diu-diu* (as in *duet)* or *doe-doe-doe*.

(4) The *hollow bell (Hohlklingel)* moves at a slow pace, in stages. The vowels of the hollow bell are *iu, oe,* and *oo ("doodle");* the consonant is *l.* Vowel and consonant must be of equal clarity in this tour. No other basic tour has seen such decisive improvement over the past decades as the hollow bell in the song of the Roller canary. Good hollow bells

1 and **2.** The gold or yellow lizard is still the most common of this breed. **3.** When the ground color is white, the color variety produced is called the blue lizard. **4.** This red lizard bears the red factor, which is evident as an orange tint in the plumage. Photo 1 by H.V. Lacey, photos 2, 3 and 4 by Vogelpark Walsrode.

←**1**

sound something like this: *liuliuliuliu* or *loeloeloeloe* or *loolooloo*. When the vowels are *ee ("bee")* or *iu,* the tour in German is called *Klingtour* (bell tour).

The basic tours just described have been introduced in their ideal forms so that the layman too gets an idea of the main components.

It goes without saying that these basic tours may also be delivered in a number of variations in respect to their sound. When this is the case, the variation tends to be a flattening of the tour. Instead of being sung with the vowels *iu, oe,* and *oo,* it is delivered as *ee, aa ("baa"),* or *ay ("day")*. As a result it is less pleasant to the ear.

Purity of song is, indeed, a decisive factor when it comes to judging and awarding of points. Valuable points are lost if a tour sounds nasal or, worse still, if it is delivered in a hoarse or squashed voice. An inadequate performance need not necessarily be due to poor hereditary material or inability. The bird needs to be only a little bit out of sorts for its voice to change. Sick birds stop singing anyway. Along with purity of tone, the dynamics of the voice are of great importance to the judges of canary song. A soft melodious performance makes a favorable impression. If, on the other hand, the bird sings with too thin and low a voice, its song will not be powerful enough. The volume is too low if the keeper cannot hear his canary when he is in the next room. If one has to come quite close to the cage to hear the song clearly, then the bird is simply not singing loudly enough. Unfortunately, some breeders disagree with this and reserve the highest praise for the bird with the softest song. The serious disadvantage of this is that such delicate-voiced stock is unlikely to produce offspring of the best quality, as a certain degree of vitality and hardiness has obviously been lost. Particularly where such delicate domestic animals like canaries are concerned, it is the breeder's responsibility to ensure they keep their natural vitality. Only then are the birds able—physically as well as in other respects—to enjoy a healthy and happy life in our homes and, through their song, to give pleasure to their owners for at least 10 years.

Apart from the basic tours described above, the repertoire of the *Edelroller* includes a few other passages, supplementary tours. These are the water roll *(Wasserrolle),* the *Glucke,* and the *Schockel*. The water roll is closely related to the *Glucke*. In earlier days—notably in the middle of the previous century, in the Harz Mountains—these tours could be heard quite frequently.

The quest for pure hollow-bass strains and the cultivation of purity in the four basic tours have increasingly led to the suppression of water roll and glucke. This applies particularly to the last few decades. The Harz Mountain Roller of 100 years ago did not yet have the clear and

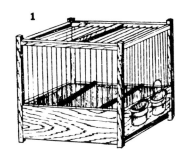

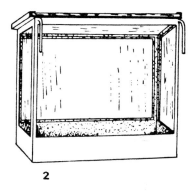

1. A small cage (24 x 15 x 18 cm) called a Harz Mountain cage is used for the training and competition of song canaries. 2. This detachable box-like bathing compartment should be sufficiently large to allow a canary to move comfortably inside. 3. The panels between the compartments in this system of cages can be pulled out when a much larger compartment is desired. The technique of moving a bird into a show cage is also seen here. Photo by H. V. Lacey.

3

pure hollow-roll song of the present day. Its song was wilder, more primitive. It was comprised of a host of passages which, while adding a lot more variety to the song, also made it impure. At that time, as a matter of fact, people went as far as to talk about two different breeding lines, one being the glucke birds and the other the roller birds.

Unfortunately the "Gluckers," as they were known for short, had a tendency to pervert their song. New generations wove shrill, inarticulate passages into their song which were painful to listen to. The same applies to the water tours, which proved equally impossible to stabilize into clearly definable cultivated tours. Another example of a "lost" tour, the *Koller* tour, remains a myth to the present day. It was said to have had a triad. Unfortunately, while there were numerous descriptions of this sound structure, no breeder or judge at any of the bigger shows ever managed to procure a bird that was able to perform the *Koller*. (When I go on to describe the Belgian Waterslager I shall treat the original passages in canary song in a little more detail.)

The *Schockel* is a very rare tour in the repertoire of a Roller canary. It is quite strenuous to deliver (as are the basic tours) in the deep pitch so greatly sought after. The Schockel is delivered at a very slow pace, usually at a constant or falling pitch. It sounds something like *hiu-hiu-hiu-hiu* or *hoe-hoe-hoe-hoe* or *ha-ha-ha* or, possibly *hoo-hoo-hoo*. It is particularly pleasant to the ear—and popular—if performed at a falling pitch: *hiu-hiu-hoe-hoe-hoo-hoo*.

The bird *expels* the Schockel; the notes form deep inside the chest. This, in fact, helps to differentiate it from the hollow bell, which is sometimes performed slowly and drawn-out and sounds similar. A bird singing the hollow bell forms the notes inside the throat. With the Schockel this is never the case—the bird emits the sound from deep inside the chest, and its body moves more or less in tune with the tour.

It is unlikely that the *Edelroller* stock of any breeder is able to sing every tour there is, let alone sing it perfectly. After all, the breeder's art is to create birds with a certain characteristic timbre of voice that is unique to his stock and differentiates it from that of other breeders. Although only very fine nuances are involved, they are readily perceived by judges and breeders. What is important above all is that the bird's song is always pure and pleasant to listen to and that the voice is of sufficient volume. To the hobbyist who buys himself a pet canary it does not really matter all that much how many points the bird can expect for one tour or another. He is advised to listen to the song of several birds and then to choose the one that appeals to him the most, basing his decision solely on personal preference. In spite of all the training and discipline these little singers are subjected to, they are not robots after all but living creatures. Today they sing like this, tomorrow perhaps quite differently. The breeders and judges are perfectly well aware of this, too, and they know that a great deal of luck is as essential as skill in a contest. The one thing that really matters is that the keeper derives pleasure from his little pet. And when the bird delivers its song we should spare a grateful thought for the many breeders who, over all those years, devoted their love, time, and energy to the task of "spiriting" such a sophisticated, skillful song out of the feathered throat. Incidentally, in Germany the term "song canary" always refers to birds of the *Edelroller* variety.

THE WATERSLAGER

While in the Harz Mountains breeders were cultivating the hollow-roll birds, foreign breeders took a fancy to other song passages and endeavored to perfect these by selective breeding. All in all, in Belgium and most especially in Mechelen and the surrounding area, breeders produced a particular variety of their own. These birds do not emit that pure and deep "cultured" song we know from the Roller variety. Their strength lies in the versatility of their voice; a repertoire consisting of 17 different tours has been listed. It is, of course, impossible in a book of this scope to describe all these passages. I shall confine myself to providing a general introduction to the song of the Waterslagers. In Germany these birds were for a long time ignored. Here, the *Edelroller* alone was regarded as the true singer among all the different song canaries. My little book is the first work in the German-language literature on canaries to introduce the Belgian song canary. It has long since ceased to be confined to its original Flemish range. The bird is not only popular in Belgium; breeders in Holland and France have long since founded breeding societies of their own for this variety, and they meet for annual contests. Due to the ever-deepening international connections and contacts among the breeders of many countries, the Waterslager has been winning an increasing number of supporters. Thus, a separate branch for this song variety has sprung up within the *Confederation Ornithologique Mondiale.* This breed has seen a heavy boost in its distribution, particularly in Italy, the U.S.A., and South Africa, as well as in South America. The demand for Waterslagers in 1968 came to a total of 100,000 birds. That is quite a lot, considering how long the Waterslagers had been leading a quiet, anonymous existence well away from the bustle of popularity that affected so many other canary varieties.

One romantic aspect has, however, remained to these birds: every Sunday the breeders come to the bird markets, as they have always done

1. These individual cages for rollers are stacked to save space. However, if necessary each cage can be moved elsewhere easily. Photo by L. van der Meid. **2.** A baby roller. Good appearance is desirable, but the pedigree and the later training of a song canary are more important. Photo by H.V. Lacey.

in Belgium, and offer their Mecheleners for sale, along with other varieties of birds. This charming custom has survived in Liege, in Brussels, and in Antwerp. The bird market is as much a part of Sunday as the ringing of the bells. The heated arguments about quality and prices of the birds that take place there between traders and customers, not infrequently in raised voices, have to be heard to be believed. The bird fancier may wish to keep these markets in mind and perhaps decide to spend a holiday in Belgium some day to pay them a visit. They have a peculiar charm of their own which only people who are really "crazy about birds" can fully appreciate and which, to them, is totally irresistible. Anyone wishing to visit the bird market must get there early in the morning, however, as it finishes at noon. The most famous bird market in Europe, of course, is the one in Paris behind Notre Dame Cathedral. It, too, is held on Sunday mornings and is the obligatory Sunday morning walk for many Parisians. It is open every week, even in winter.

The age of this variety is given as 300 years by Belgian authors. But this must be seen for what it is: a guess. Any information older than 100 years about the evolution and early days of this breed is unclear and hazy in its transmission. This is not really surprising, since no partially reliable canary literature—telling us about the evolution of a variety—was published before 1850. Be that as it may, the Belgians have been breeding canaries for many centuries, and the posture varieties originate from that country as well. The Waterslager, along with the *Edelroller,* must be evolutionarily the most advanced variety. Waterslager (or Mechelener Waterslager) is, of course, the name given to it in its native country, but its French name *Canari de chant Malinois* or simply *Malinois* is widely used, too. It means Mechelener song canary or just Mechelener.

I have so far omitted to say what an excellent mimic the canary is among the finches. Mimics, in the bird world, are species that imitate the voices of other species. This makes it very important that canary males have good teachers in their youth. What they do, more or less successfully, is to try and imitate the song they hear and the voices of their elders. If young canary males are, for example, placed in the same room as a singing linnet, one will be astonished just how quickly and accurately the canaries learn its piping song, which will then stay with them for the rest of their lives. The song of other finches is picked up with equal ease. Father Brehm, the "bird pastor," taught ordinary canaries the song of the tree pipit. The voice of the nightingale has delighted bird lovers from time immemorial, and it will surprise no one that canary breeders have attempted to teach their little singers the sounds made by this "queen of song."

The Belgian Waterslagers have a sob-like quality about their voice which in some stocks clearly shows the resemblance to the voice of the nightingale. In the twenties a breeder from Bremen, Carl Reich, succeeded in producing his own variety of "nightingale canaries" after two decades of hard work. What he did was to provide his young males with real nightingales as "teachers." This was a great achievement, particularly in view of the training period of the young canaries, considering that the two species have their molting as well as their song season at very different times of the year. Unfortunately, these birds did not survive World War II and must be regarded as extinct. In Italy, independently of these German efforts, there have also been attempts to teach canaries the nightingale's song and to breed it into them. But nothing more has been heard about this for the past 10 years.

The main ingredient of the Waterslager's song is, of course, the *waterslag*. It may be delivered in three different stages. The Flemish breeders have been using some marvellously phonetic language to denote the individual tours. I shall use the original Flemish terms here, saving myself longwinded descriptions.

Right at the top, in terms of points awarded and popularity, is the *klokkende waterslag* which may begin with the consonants *bl, gl, kl,* and *l.* It sounds something like this: *blooee-blooee-blooee-blooee-gloo! gloo! klok! klok! klok!* The vowels *aa, ee, ay,* and *iu* give this tour a certain hardness that reduces its value.

In second place is the *bollende waterslag,* which is characterized by the consonants *v, b, l, g,* and very rarely, *d* as well. The vowels are the same as above. The tour sounds roughly like this: *voo-voo-voo! loo-loo-loo! bo-bo-bo!* The sound should be kept low, at an even pitch, and the beat must not be too powerful, but calm and lingering.

For both these tours the bird needs a great deal of air. The posture of a singing Waterslager is, therefore, quite different from that of a Roller.

The third kind of waterslag is of lesser importance. This is the *rollende waterslag,* called *rol* (roll) for short by the breeders. It sounds like a water roll in the repertoire of an *Edelroller.* The consonants of this tour are *l* and *v.* The vowels most commonly used are again *iu, oe,* and *oo.* The vowel *aa* is considered a fault; it greatly detracts from the tour's value. If the consonants and vowels I have just mentioned are combined, we hear the following variations: *looloolooloolooloo! viuviuviuviuviuviu! lololololo!* This passage is sung at a slightly higher pitch than the two preceding tours. The timbre is harder and usually louder as well. If the performance is lacking in strength, the singing generally continues longer. Very high pitch, along with a colorless and hard delivery, entails loss of points. It is important that the roll is sung

1. Gravel (also called grit) of a size suitable for canaries is readily available. 2. Canary and rape seeds are the main components of commercial canary mixes. 3. A busy person with very few canaries may find it more convenient to buy prepared rearing and conditioning food instead of mixing the formula himself. 4. A fixed routine for feeding is recommended. The nutritional needs of a canary are discussed fully in the text. Photo by H.V. Lacey.

4

with a closed beak. Only then does it possess the dignity and purity of the soprano part in the Waterslager's repertoire.

Unlike the *Edelroller,* the Waterslager does not sing all the tours of its song with a closed beak. The whole timbre of its voice is harsher and louder than the Roller's. Consequently, certain passages of its song sound entirely different as well.

The *Chorr* and *Knorr* are the bass tours in the Waterslager's song. In these passages the bird reaches the lowest pitch it is capable of. The sound structure is very similar to what we are familiar with from the *Edelroller,* except that the tour is harsher in character, phonetically less soft. The first syllable of *chorr* resembles the guttural *ch,* as in Scottish *loch* or German *kochen* or *machen.* It is the opening consonant of the tour, so we hear something like *chorr-chorr-chorr-chorr! churr-churr-churr-churr!* A very similar variation is the *knorr,* which starts with the consonants *kn* and again ends with *r.* The consonant at the end may be held for a while, sounding like this: *knor-r-r-r-r-r-r-r! knur-r-r-r-r-r-r-r-r!* The rhythmical movement of the tour may be falling, or rising and falling several times. This sounds more complicated on paper than it does to the ear when the bird is performing. Both tours must be delivered with a closed beak. If the bird opens its beak during these passages, the singing becomes a highly unpleasant rattle.

The staaltonen (steel tones, also referred to as *tjonker* or *tjonks)* are the oddest sounds emitted by the Waterslager. This tour is said to come closest to the song of the nightingale. If we remind ourselves that the individual tours have been given onomatopoeic names, we can hear in the word *tjonk* a resemblance to the sobbing quality of the nightingale's song. Alternatively, this tour could be described as a double-tone sung at brief intervals. It sounds like a hammer on an anvil. This tour is very attractive and is the one most characteristic of this canary variety. The consonants are *t* or *tj* at the beginning and *ng* or *nk* at the end. The vowels are *oe, oo,* and *ee.* If the vowel sounds are like *iu, aa, eh ("depth"),* or *ui ("Buick"),* this detracts from their value. Such a tour loses its characteristic sound and becomes less pleasant to listen to. Pure *tjonker* of a high quality go like this: *teeng! teeng! teeng! toong! toong! toong! tjoenk! tjoenk! tjoenk! toeng! toeng! toeng! tjoong! tjoong! tjoong! tjoonk! tjoonk! tjoonk!*

The steel tones may be delivered at any musical pitch but must always be sung clearly and distinctly by the bird. The varying pitch also results in a varying number of points awarded. Very rare but highly desirable is this tour at a rising or falling pitch. The *tjonker* are sung with an open beak; only then does the double-tone character of this tour come fully into its own.

The flutes and their variation, the so-called *soeten* (pronounced *zooten*), are not confined to the Waterslager; these sounds are produced by almost any canary. Even color canary males include them in their repertoire. They are part of the original, natural, canary song. Although fairly closely related to the flutes as sung by the *Edelroller,* this tour does not attain the latter's rich, warm depth of sound. It is flatter and sharper, although some birds of the Waterslager variety are able to articulate their flutes at a deep pitch, which sounds very pleasing. I must, however, strongly advise against crossing these two song varieties with each other, as this would lead to the loss of the best qualities in the songs of each.

There are also other, less important, tours in the song of the Waterslager: *woeten* (pronounced *vooten*), *bellen* (bell tour), *belrol* (bell roll), and *fluitenrol* (flute roll). There is also an independent *tjokkenrol*, which alternatively may be spoken about as *Tjokken*. Over and above this, a *schockel*—in the form of a water schockel—may be heard, as well as a *glucke* and a *lach tour* (laughing tour). Finally, one may come across a type of water roll (not, however, to be confused with the waterslag; this is a mixed rolling tour of lesser importance).

Like the *Edelroller,* the Waterslager too may lose points for a number of listed faults such as unpleasing ringing passages, usually delivered in a shrill, harsh voice, and *Hard aufzug.* As already pointed out, these faults are really only of interest to the breeder. The hobbyist does not think of them as ruining a bird's song. He can however, seek the advice of a breeder or some other experienced person if he, too, wishes to acquire a deeper understanding of the analysis of canary song.

If one wanted to give a brief comparative description of the songs of the *Edelroller* and the Waterslager, one would label the latter's repertoire as more primitive, more varied, and louder, with harsh, metallic sounds. To the expert the Waterslager's song is simply wilder. The *Edelroller* delivers its song more softly; the most characteristic component is the rolling, which goes on for a long time, and the soft piping. Furthermore, the *Edelroller's* performance has a quieter rhythm. Waterslagers of the Belgian variety are bred exclusively in a pure yellow color (of which "straw" is an apt description). The males have a more intense color than the females, the latter being pale to almost whitish yellow. Small spots, provided they do not exceed one centimeter in diameter, or a dark wing feather are tolerated. A bird with more dark spots or a larger dark area cannot be regarded as pure. In fact, in a case like this bird cross-breeding with *Edelrollers* will automatically be suspected. The Mecheleners are, generally speaking, more than one centimeter longer and have a larger skeleton as well.

Left: Cuttlebone is a good source of minerals which should be part of a canary's diet. *Below:* This canary is ready to leave the nest and will be moved to its own cage. The cage and breeding equipment are then scrupulously cleaned for the next breeding. Photo by L. Hess.

Managing Canaries

THE CAGE

Research into animal behavior has long since established that the concept of imprisonment as understood by us human beings is virtually meaningless in the animal world. Prof. Hediger has proved scientifically that an animal which has come under human care immediately makes itself at home in what it considers to be its territory. This applies particularly to species that have been living exclusively under man's care for generations and also breed in captivity. Thus the cage our canary lives in is really its home, and the bird feels sheltered and secure inside it. Unfortunately, in spite of the multitude of cages available, only a few really good models (adapted to the bird's requirements) are found on the market even today. The argument for useful and good bird cages has been going on for almost ninety years. The grandmaster of aviculture,

K. Russ, already in 1872 spoke out vehemently against fancy cages. Such cages, cluttered up with all sorts of intricate ornaments and useless decor, not only seriously restricted the bird's movement, but with their nooks and crannies also served as ideal breeding places for parasites. Nor are they easy to clean, and the inmates of such prisons are difficult to see. One's gaze is lured away from the bird because the cage itself pushes into the foreground. Most modern cages, unhappily, have to be rejected as too small. It almost looks as though the manufacturer's sole aim, in designing and producing them, had been cheapness. What to the eye seems an elegant and pleasing arrangement of lines (as it is indeed described in the advertisements) almost invariably turns out to mean very restricted space for the feathered occupant. A length of 40 cm is an absolute minimum for a canary cage; a smaller length should never be considered. Many of the common commercial cages show a nicely shaped rounding-off extending over 40 cm, but for the bird there is really very little room. The bottom area is almost always smaller than the cage dimensions quoted; this is something the buyer should be aware of.

Canaries are lively animals for which, as for all birds, exercise is vital. Above all it is important that they are able to use their wings. For this reason, the perches inside the cage should be apart far enough for the birds to have to use their wings in order to get from one to the next. For the same reason, the perches must not be fitted too close to the roof of the cage. Exaggerating slightly, a cage can never be big enough! In practice this means it is good for the bird to be allowed to leave its cage for a few hours and fly about in greater freedom inside the room. Canaries can readily be let loose in this way once we have tamed and trained them to return to their cages voluntarily.

If a canary is treated calmly and unhurriedly at all times, it will soon develop a certain amount of trust in its keeper. The bird quickly learns who fills up its food trough and slips it the occasional tid-bit. This growth of trust can be speeded up by depriving the bird of food for an hour. After the daily cleaning of the cage the feeding trough is taken out for an hour and the cage is left open so that the bird is free to fly about in the room. The bird can be relied upon never to take its eye off the cage and to instantly notice when the food container appears in the keeper's hand. Without any hasty movements but making sure that the bird is watching, the keeper puts the trough in its usual place in the cage. The bird will find this impossible to resist and will go back inside its house. Discreetly and with as natural an air as possible the keeper closes the door behind the bird, but always without any hasty movement!

With similar methods it is also possible to get the bird to sit on one's finger or hand. Hour-long removal of food must not, of course, degenerate into ruthlessly letting the bird starve. In that way one would achieve nothing. The handling of birds requires a calm, even-tempered disposition on the part of the keeper. This is what makes the hobby such a nerve tonic.

Nervous, hasty, and uncontrolled abrupt movements in humans are not liked by any animal. The secret of a good animal-and-bird keeper is that he has his feelings under control at all times; it is this self-discipline that makes the animals trust him. A properly tamed bird comes to the keeper voluntarily—this should be our goal. We must never reach out for the bird with the hand. If we suddenly grab the bird, its distrust in us will last for a long time. For the small bird that human hand suddenly grasping it is a dangerous predator. However, once an absolute trust has been allowed to build up, the hand too will cease to alarm the bird. Indeed, the cocks chosen by the breeder to serve several hens are only too anxious to be picked up and they start singing while in the hand as they are moved from one wedding to the next.

A good canary cage should have a length of 40 cm and its length should exceed its height, and its height its depth. A cage of these dimensions is suitable for the solitary singer. A pair, which perhaps one intends to breed, needs a cage with a minimum length of 50 cm. A simple rectangular shape is not only timeless but also more attractive than anything else where a bird cage is concerned. However, if for any reason the bird fancier has to make do with a smaller cage for his canary, then he must let the bird fly about freely in the room for at least an hour each day. The best time for this exercise is in the afternoon or early evening: first, because most hobbyists have to go to work and are therefore unable to let the bird have its hour of freedom in the morning, and secondly, because the canary generally devotes the morning to practicing its song. Lastly, the bird should receive its food at exactly the same time every day. Late afternoon or early evening is ideal for this if the bird remains in a lighted room. The canary then fills its crop for the night and will feed on the remaining seeds in the morning. Every canary has its favorite seed, and this is the first to get picked out from among the mixture we offer it. But more about that is discussed in the chapter on feeding.

Ideally, a cage in the home should be placed at eye level. Birds are creatures of the air, consequently they do not feel comfortable in surroundings where they are constantly being towered over by other creatures. If the cage is simply put on a table somewhere, we human beings seem like large, dangerous monsters to the birds as we move

1. Fluffed feathers when seen in an otherwise normally sleek-looking bird should always be investigated. The condition could mean that illness is present. Photo by L. van der Meid. 2. This frilled canary is not in molt. In this breed the curling of certain feathers is normal. Note the unmodified feathers of the variegated canary on the right.

around the cage. The best place for a bird cage remains the wall, especially a spot that is reached by the sun for a few hours each day.

In some cases lack of space may make it impossible to hang up the cage in a sunny spot. Then the sympathetic bird fancier compromises by simply putting the cage on the window sill when the sun shines. This need not be done every day, of course, but the sun undoubtedly makes a difference! For example, let's assume this is a day in April and we have opened the window, so the bird in its cage is able to enjoy to the fullest the warm rays of the sun. It ruffles up the feathers, spreads out the wings, and subjects the greatest possible surface area to the sunshine.

The warning "beware of drafts" will be given by every experienced bird keeper. Nothing is as dangerous for the canary as drafts. In fact, if the bird gets away with nothing more serious than an untimely molt it has had a lucky escape. When hanging up the cage, then, the keeper must make absolutely sure the chosen spot cannot be reached by harmful drafts. Whether the cagestands that have become so popular today are an entirely desirable accessory to bird keeping I hesitate to say. Admittedly, in the home they are nice to look at, even decorative, but when it comes to animal psychology the place on the wall is much better since the bird feels much safer there. The closed wall at the back of the cage offers a great deal of security, whereas in an entirely exposed cage the bird will feel threatened from all directions.

Round cages are completely unsuitable. The birds' orientation in space, just like our own, relies wholly on lines of demarcation visible to the eye. For this reason any space with lines of demarcation which surround the bird vertically and horizontally is much more pleasant than being confined in a circular cage. Whichever way the bird turns, it finds itself enclosed everywhere by the same curved cage wall. Another disadvantage of most of these tower-type cages is that they are much too narrow and cramped; the movement of the occupant is severely restricted.

For the purpose of training young male canaries, breeders use small song cages of a special design. These cages, *Harzer Bauerchen,* as they are known in Germany, are the brain-child of a canary breeder from the Harz Mountains and date back to the previous century. They are necessary in order to give the bird a certain amount of schooling. Generally speaking, the males are shut up inside these small song cages for three months.

Unfortunately these cages are often exceedingly small. The minimum length should be 25 cm, at least enabling the bird to turn around without difficulty and allowing short jumps from perch to perch. Birds from flight cages are in much better breeding condition, having been able to move about freely all through the molting period and the winter right into the breeding season. Not even the best food can compensate for lack of movement. The condition of the musculature, the entire metabolism, plumage, and posture—to sum up, the bird as a whole benefits from being able to use its wings for a few months, from exercising in more or less the same way as when free in the wild.

In this respect the birdhouse with attached aviaries is ideal for canaries too. While this does not apply unreservedly to all varieties and to every stage in the annual cycle, broadly speaking the advantages of an aviary for canaries as much as for other birds are obvious. Nowhere else can the bird enjoy bathing, air and sun, flight and rest to the same extent as it can in a large aviary. With respect to canaries there is, however, one reservation; trouble may result when a bigger flock is kept in one room. The males attack each other with great ferocity. Fierce fighting goes on inside the aviary almost all the time. Although serious injuries are rare, the negative side of these battles between rivals cannot be overlooked. Gradually a certain hierarchy comes into being. Although this may not be clearly defined or rigidly adhered to, it will eventually result in some of the males finding themselves firmly at the bottom of the pecking order where (to exaggerate slightly) they are hardly allowed as much as to breathe. They always sit in the farthest corner, dare not sing anymore, and are allowed near the feeding trough only after everyone else, and then only if no dominant male is around. It is important, therefore, to remember this aggressive streak in our canaries and avoid keeping too many males in the same enclosure. Where partitions or similar objects block the view and prevent a constant confrontation between the males, the matter is less serious—then the battles are not nearly so fierce and embittered. All the cages supplied for the home nowadays are provided with a base that is closed on all sides and contains the food troughs. Seed husks, sand, and loose feathers are thus prevented from flying about in the room and annoying the housewife.

How does the canary react to being kept in a community cage? Usually, of course, people acquire a single songster, since, as already mentioned, too many members of this species should not be kept together. There remains the question of how the bird would do in a bigger cage with other species. Basically, all members of the finch family would be suitable, provided they do not disturb the canary's song. As soon as another male finch mixes its wild song into the tours of the *Edelroller* the fine melting softness of the latter's performance is drowned. Associating the canary with budgerigars is out of the question since parakeets have an entirely different behavior pattern, a completely different language. They do not understand the threat and defense

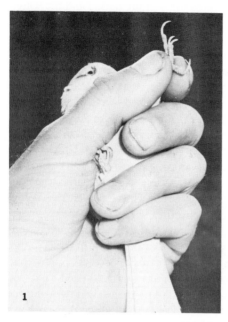

1. The claws of canaries frequently become overgrown. When they reach this length, they should be trimmed with nail clippers or scissors. **2.** Some breeders carefully trim the feathers around the vent to ensure fertilization. **3, 4.** Note the open baskets which contain these canary nests. When using any fine nesting material, be sure the strands are short enough that the birds' feet cannot become entangled.

2

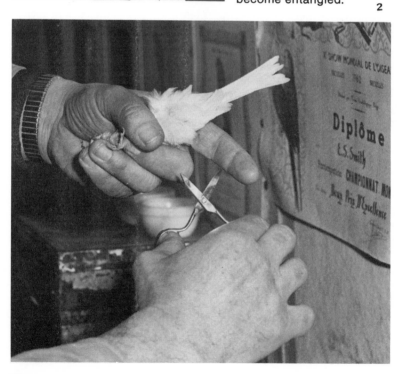

3

4

postures the canary adopts, and because they do not understand they cruelly attack it. A canary attacked by a budgerigar in courting mood can suffer a great deal of damage.

Distant relatives such as the gray singing finch, the green singing finch, and indeed all African serins, may under certain circumstances be suitable as fellow lodgers. The keeper must, however, always make sure that the birds really get along together.

FOODS AND FEEDING

Anyone who decides to keep a pet for his enjoyment also takes on the responsibility for the well-being of his charge. Where canaries are concerned, this is neither an expensive nor a time-consuming business. Nevertheless, it should not be neglected with the often cited excuse that perhaps canaries are undemanding. In nature there is no such thing as undemanding or demanding. Free-living animal species always fit fully into their environment, are fully integrated, and the hunt for food, the search for a territory, territorial defense, the selection of their food, and all the other patterns of behavior are nothing more than rational components of a complex network scientists have termed ecology. A bird that has been domesticated, like the canary, for example, has completely lost touch with its original environment. Man is now looking after it and providing it with suitable food every day. What the keeper needs to bear in mind, however, is the fact that a canary's way of life is much more strongly governed by the natural cycle of the seasons than man's. An example of this is the molt which occurs every year for the replacement of the bird's plumage. This most striking phenomenon of a natural cycle is perhaps one of the most obvious to the layman. But the molt is only a part of the annual cycle that influences the biology of the canary. It should, therefore, be perfectly clear to every thinking canary fancier that the little bird cannot be expected to remain fit and well if for years its diet, which often consists of nothing but dry seeds, stays exactly the same.

Before we go on to discuss the different types of food and diet ingredients for canaries in more detail, I would like to draw the reader's attention to an important fact: anyone who has bought himself a young canary will find that with every successive molt the bird grows lazier with respect to its singing. Most hobbyists experience this, and the question as to why this is so must be the one most frequently asked in canary keeping. The answer, alas, is just one ominous word that could be applied to countless humans as well: overeating!

Most of the commercial brands of food mixtures are extremely rich, and what endangers the pets is the laziness of their owners. Every day the food hopper is emptied and filled up again, the keeper not bothering to check whether any particular seeds are left uneaten by the bird. All birds supplied with mixed food first of all pick out those components they like best. In the case of canaries these are hemp, niger, lettuce, maw, and linseed, depending on what they feel like eating and the quality of the harvest. As a result the vast majority of canaries kept in the home receive a diet with far too high a fat content and therefore quickly come to suffer from obesity which sooner or later kills them off.

There is no reason why the bird should not receive a nutritious seed mix. On the contrary, it is all to the good. What is absolutely vital, however, is that a regular feeding time be introduced and strictly adhered to. Best suited are either late afternoon or early evening. Then the bird picks out the seeds it likes best. The next morning the food trough is taken out and lightly shaken and the empty seed husks are blown off the top. What remains, as a rule, is the round, brownish-red rape seed (the "bread" of canaries), together with a little canary seed. This is put back into the cage and by the afternoon it will have disappeared almost completely. However, a small amount should always be there; then the keeper can be quite sure that his bird gets enough to eat. Keepers who take pride in pointing out that their birds have invariably emptied the seed hopper by feeding time are bad hosts. That the animals' tastes change should not be forgotten either. What they fancy today may be left untouched tomorrow. To find some left-overs in the food trough is, therefore, quite normal. But one should examine the remaining seeds to find out which ones the bird declines. It is just possible that this particular variety of seed is inedible. Bad harvests can happen, and all too often seeds that are unfit for consumption are still added to the mixture and sold.

In previous centuries the word "host" was used quite a lot in Germany to denote an animal fancier or keeper. If one thinks about the meaning of this term one must admit it was certainly apt. A good host looks after the physical well-being of his guests; he finds a happy medium, offering neither too little nor too much.

A good mixture consists of the following:

Rape   is considered the canaries' daily bread, particularly with regard to songsters. Good rape should be nicely granular and sweet to the taste. Nowadays no breeder omits to test the flavor himself by biting through a few seeds with the incisors and testing the nut-sweet aroma with the tip of the tongue. Rape that tastes rancid and bitter is unsuitable as canary food.

Canary has been a major component of all canary foods from the earliest days. As already mentioned, the wild birds on the Canary

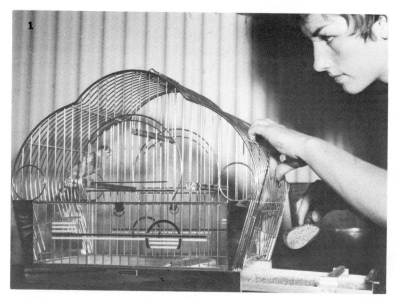

1. The sand or grit must be replaced regularly to remove uneaten food and waste material. Photo by L. van der Meid. 2. A wooden perch can be scraped clean and then sanded. Photo by L. van der Meid. 3. A medicine dropper is the best equipment for administering small amounts of liquid (medicine, oils, vitamins, etc.).

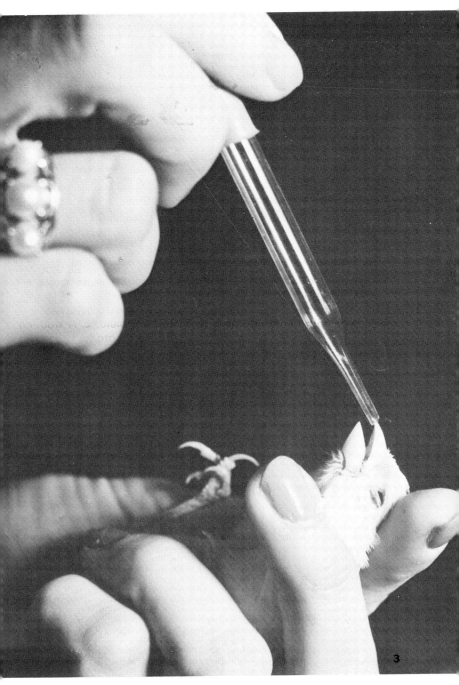

3

Islands are partial to it too. Today there are many different varieties. That from Morocco is the best—it is always fully granular and properly ripened. Unfortunately, this is not always true of canary seed grown in Europe (Italy, for example). If it is not ripe it has a lingering smell and a gray appearance. If in doubt, a germination test will help to assess the quality of the seeds. Large-scale breeders who buy their canary food unmixed and by the ton have to apply spot-check germination tests anyway if they want to be sure of getting food in perfect condition. For the hobbyist this is, on the whole, neither possible nor necessary. By and large, modern transport, connections and the considerable competition in the animal-food trade guarantee good quality.

Niger was for a long time held in low esteem in canary nutrition. Unjustly so, for this compositae is quite popular with the birds and nutritionally of value too, like most food plants of this group. Niger should, however, be given in moderation as its fat content is comparatively high.

Hemp is a somewhat controversial ingredient of mixtures. It has a very high fat content and should only be used when freshly harvested. In the nutrition of song canaries it is only of minor importance, but the breeders of other types of canaries cannot do without it. Hemp is particularly useful in the winter, as well as before and during the breeding season. It gives the birds energy and helps in getting them into breeding condition. Some breeders prefer to offer it daily, freshly ground in small quantities, as the husks are often so hard that the canaries are unable to open them.

Linseed, lettuce, poppy, sometimes *cabbage* too, are supplementary ingredients found only in minor quantities in the mix. The same applies to *oats,* although the posture canaries get these in greater amounts. Anyone wishing to enrich the mixture need not hesitate to add millet seeds of various kinds. Although millet is not among the most popular canary foods, as a supplement to breeding food it is excellent, especially when germinated.

The extensive range of seeds on the market nowadays, from all over the world, offers incomparably more possibilities to formulate a suitable mixture than was the case a few decades ago. This also explains why these mixtures have not been described in the older literature on canaries.

Tidbits, for our canaries, are extra rations in the form of fresh plant food. The pertinent green plants (including, above all, weeds) will be discussed in more detail in a later section. An occasional small lettuce leaf is also a welcome treat. Use caution with commercial lettuce, however—it may have been treated with chemicals. This is harmful not only to the canary but to all other cage birds as well and may have fatal consequences. Spinach, dandelion, a little piece of carrot, or sweet apple, orange, and grapefruit in small pieces are tidbits that are always appreciated, although, of course, the bird will have to get to know them and get used to them first. In the evening this supplementary food must always be taken out of the cage so that no wilted, rotten, or (worse still) moldy left-overs can endanger the bird's health. When feeding lettuce we must make sure it is never wet. While some birds can tolerate wet lettuce quite well, others have died as a result of it. How well greenstuff as a whole is tolerated depends on whether the birds are used to it. A bird that gets greenfood only at irregular intervals, and then in large quantities, is more at risk than one that is used to receiving a small portion of greenstuff every day.

A small clip-on food container should never be absent from the cage. It is used for egg-biscuit, high-energy food, or molt diet, etc. A can of high-energy food for canaries should really be kept in reserve by everyone, and it will do no harm to fill the clip-on container with it once or twice a week. Constantly supplementing the bird's seed mix with a commercial high-energy food is not advisable. A small piece of toast pushed through the bars or some cake or biscuit crumbs will do no harm. Our own meals should, however, not be shared with the bird, no matter how much the canary may desire this. The odd sugar cube is not good for our pet either. The canary is, after all, a seed-eater by nature, and its digestive organs are not equipped to break down such foods without suffering damage.

Dealers now offer practical containers for food and water, either for individual birds or in larger sizes for a number of birds, which can hold supplies for several days. These automatic food dispensers should at last manage to convince people that owning a canary does not mean one can never leave the house even for a day. Such food dispensers are of a fairly simple, no-nonsense design. They store food for about three days.

THE MOLT IS NOT A DISEASE

The feathers wear out in all birds. An annual replacement is therefore necessary, and nature has arranged this for all birds, including the canary. The molting period, as the time of this feather change is called, in the canary happens to be in late summer and early fall. The main molt takes place in August and September. Young birds in their first year of life replace only the contour feathers, not the large flight and steering feathers in the wings and tail. A complete replacement of the feathers takes place only after the second year of life.

The molt is a trying time for all birds, and they prefer to spend it in

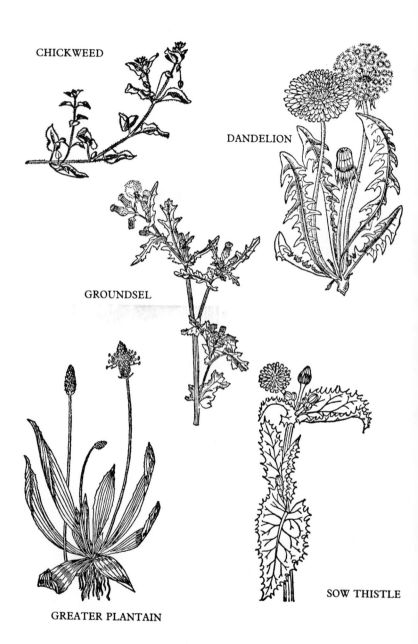

CHICKWEED

DANDELION

GROUNDSEL

GREATER PLANTAIN

SOW THISTLE

2

3

1. Some food plants for canaries. **2.** The mineral block or cuttlebone should be within easy reach of a canary. There are special holders for placing the block on the wall of a cage, away from the floor where it can be soiled. Photo by L. van der Meid. **3.** Dandelion is a very common weed found in many places, but it is important that only very clean samples be offered to canaries. Photo by G. Pickow.

← **1**

relative seclusion. This makes sense when one considers that during this period their flight ability is, of course, impaired to a greater or lesser degree and the feathers fail to give complete protection. On the other hand, while the molting period puts a certain amount of stress on the bird, it is most certainly not a disease!

During the molt the canary does not sing. At this stage in the bird's cycle, food which is high in nutrients and vitamins is of special importance. Minerals, above all, promote quick, smooth feather replacement. In the past the so-called molting-salt was widely praised for its powers, but we now have available a whole range of balanced preparations that are specifically adapted to the requirements of molting birds.

The molt takes about 6 weeks. The end is in sight once the pinfeathers (the closed sheaths of the newly-sprouting feathers) have appeared on the head and neck. Soon, in roughly two weeks' time, the bird will resume its singing. Plenty of greenstuff, including half-ripe seeds, should supplement the diet during the molting period. Equally important is the constant provision of fresh grit or other calcium additions. One example of a cheap and easily digested calcium source for canaries is the crushed shells of boiled eggs dried well in the oven.

A sleepy, listless behavior, dull eyes, fluffed-out feathers (making the bird look almost as round as a ball), a jerking tail, and noisy (squawking or rattling) breathing indicate that a bird is sick.

Today pet shops and drug stores stock a variety of drugs for the treatment of sick birds. In addition, they may well be able to offer sound advice. Modern animal medicine has made good progress and achieved good results, particularly with regard to diseases which were still considered incurable a few decades ago. Sulfonamides and antibiotics have proved excellent remedies. A book by H.-S. Raethel called *Bird Diseases* (T.F.H. Publications) offers much worthwhile information on bird care. Every bird keeper should get himself a copy long before his first bird becomes ill.

BIRD-CARE: HOW LONG DOES IT TAKE?

The hectic activity, with the hours of each working day crammed with commitments, the enforced punctuality, the multitude of environmental stimuli—these have turned us human beings into creatures who have to ask perpetually what the time is. In particular, the above applies to the populations of countries with a high standard of technology. Small wonder, then, that anyone who acquires a cage bird immediately wishes to know: how much time does such a canary require of me? In the time-pressed jargon of our modern economy the concise answer is five minutes per day, plus half an hour once a week.

The food and water containers have to be cleaned and refilled every day, preferably in the afternoon or evening. If the keeper wants to do more, he can blow the empty seed husks out of the food container the next morning (which means an additional minute per day). Once a week the cage has to be "spring-cleaned." Bowls, tray, and wire bars are cleaned with a brush and warm soapy water and dried. All nooks and crannies are scrubbed thoroughly to prevent parasites from settling in them. The perches (the original wooden ones are much to be preferred to those of plastic) are scraped all over with a knife and then washed too. Food and drinking vessels, as well as the little bird bath are cleaned in the same way. The newly washed cage is dried and the perches re-fitted securely in position so that there is no danger of collapse when the bird jumps on and off. The keeper should never economize on sand. The layer of sand need not necessarily be an inch thick, but it should cover the bottom of the cage properly. The sand is pushed against the walls and into the corners as soon as the bird flaps its wings. It is a good idea to put a sheet of paper, an ordinary cardboard or sanded paper, (the latter with the smooth side down), on the floor of the cage. This helps to keep the sand in position, and the paper soiled with feces can readily be replaced. With a little bit of practice, the whole procedure can be completed within half an hour, and the cage becomes more attractive to look at.

It would be a mistake, however, to regard this task of making one's feathered friends comfortable as work. Genuine bird lovers would not dream of calling it work in any case. Caring for birds is a recreation and a source of relaxation. The few minutes we have to devote to the maintenance of cage and accessories keep us near our birds, the hobby we have chosen.

Canaries like their bath! Unlike the budgerigar whose natural habitat is dry grassland, canaries need the opportunity to bathe. During the cooler months of the year a daily bath is not necessary, but twice a week the small bird bath should be hooked onto the bird's cage. For very little money it is possible today to get quite attractive models of translucent plastic. Nevertheless, it is a serious mistake to select a very small bathing dish just to save a few pennies. It is cruel to subject a bird to cramped bathing conditions. The bath must be big enough to allow the bird to splash about in it—canaries frequently enjoy doing that. Incidentally, there is no need for you to get worried if your pet emerges from his bath dripping wet, even if the bird looks rather "sorry for itself" in this soggy state and no longer bears much resemblance to a canary. It is vital, however, that the wet bird is not exposed to the slightest draft, or else it would almost certainly catch a chill. Bathing is particularly important during the molt, as it promotes feather replacement. There is really no reason why the little bird bath should not remain hooked to the cage permanently throughout the warmer season. As soon as the water has been changed (and this should be done twice a day), the bird promptly takes a bath.

Warnings have been expressed about cold bath water, but there is no need to be too particular in this respect. My canaries have been getting their water straight from the tap for years, and it has never done them the slightest harm. However, I suppose it depends on what the birds are used to. Birds living in warm rooms react more sensitively than do those kept in unheated rooms or even in outdoor aviaries.

Care of the canary's beak and feet must not be neglected either. The bird gets a chance to sharpen its beak if we provide a piece of cuttlebone (that is the internal shell of the cuttlefish, a type of cephalopod, collected on the shore). Especially manufactured mineral blocks serve the same purpose. By care of the feet I mean trimming the claws with a small pair of scissors or a nail clipper. To make this task easier, the bird is picked up with the left hand, and with the thumb and index finger of the same hand we hold up the bird's foot. It is best to do this against the light so that the vascular parts of the claws are easier to see. With the other hand one cuts off the tip of the claw that has grown too long. But do not cut off too much! A small piece of clear horny tissue must remain to protect the blood vessels, otherwise severe bleeding could result. Whenever possible, the trimming of the claws should be left to an experienced person.

The claws of young birds do not require cutting yet. The legs of older birds show a horny growth as well. This is not a sign of disease (like scaly leg, for example, where small parasites cause the legs to grow raised scales) but a replacement of the horny parts during the molt. The bird not only changes its feathers, but the skin, too, is replaced, and so are the horny scales on the legs and feet. Birds that have the opportunity to enjoy frequent baths usually get rid of the old horny deposit on the legs themselves. The newly grown horny scales are already underneath. If the old layer is excessively hard, it sticks to the new one. A quick cure for this is a warm footbath with water or oil, (but please use oil with care and keep it well away from the feathers!) This softens the horny bits and makes them easy to remove. Again, the bird is picked up with one hand, and the feet and legs are bathed as far as the joint with the other hand. If water is used, a fat-based skin cream should be lightly rubbed into the hardened parts afterwards. Any beauty or skin cream is suitable. A special leg cream for birds is available too. This foot cure is at most required once a year. Often, creams do not need to be applied at all if the bird has a good bottom layer in its cage, receives the correct diet, and has ample opportunities to bathe.

CHOOSING A CANARY

The layman gets confused by the multitude of varieties and colors of canaries found on the market nowadays. It is difficult to make a choice. What, then, are the criteria by which the bird fancier should select his little indoor friend? The question of usefulness does not come into it, since obviously the canary is to be a pet, a hobby, a lovable living creature to have around.

If the hobbyist's main expectation with regard to his pet is song, then he will select a male canary of a pure-bred song-bird stock. If, on the other hand, he prefers to look at a colorful bird, then he can take his pick from among the countless different color shades available. What color he chooses is immaterial and entirely a matter of personal preference. And if he does not intend to become a show breeder anyway, then a pied bird will do equally well. In fact, attractively mottled birds often sell better than specimens of uniform coloring.

I need not point out that color canaries sing just as much as do song canaries, the only difference being that their voice is less cultured. Their song sounds harsher and louder. As a matter of fact, many people prefer this type of bird song to, for example, the delicate roller tours delivered by song canaries. Furthermore, many of today's color breeders have already succeeded in crossing Rollers into their stock, thus creating birds which sing rather oddly but very pleasing passages that are no longer based exclusively on the vowel *ee*. However, as already pointed out, before committing himself, the hobbyist is advised to listen to the song of the bird he is interested in. On the other hand, the bird fancier who regards his pet as an ornament, or simply takes pleasure in its appearance, may find that one of the oddly shaped canaries is for him. Here, too, there are birds to suit every taste. There are big thin ones and short fat ones, dainty little dwarfs and stylish Frills, thin and graceful creatures and placid-looking "Beatles" with a fringe which breeders call a crest.

What is important in every case is that the bird we purchase is healthy. Canaries are lively animals which are constantly moving about. With their feathers smooth and close to the body, they hop from perch to perch and keep an attentive eye on everything that goes on in their surroundings. Smooth feathers and a lively personality are indicative of good health. The feathers around the cloaca (anal region) must not be dirty, let alone wet and matted. That points toward a disease of the digestive organs. Audible breathing, coughing, and constant shaking of

66

1. A circular cage, for reasons mentioned in the text, is not suited for keeping and training a song canary. 2. When confronted by a great array of cages in a bird shop, one could easily forget the requirements of the canary itself. Photo by Dr. H.R. Axelrod. 3. A bird cage stand may be attractive and decorative, but it is not really needed for keeping a song canary. 4. The bird room of a serious canary breeder. Note that only one side of each cage is exposed. Photo by H.V. Lacey.

3

4

the beak (as though the bird were trying to rid itself of something inside its throat) must lead one to suspect a disease of the respiratory tract. To buy such specimens is not advisable.

The best time to buy a canary is in the fall. By then the birds have completed their molt, and the selection is wider than at any other time. The young birds of that particular year have already become adult, and the older animals which had been used for breeding show themselves in their brand-new plumage. In the fall the breeders are most able to meet everyone's requirements. Although the pet trade offers canaries all the year 'round, prices are at their most favorable level during fall and early winter. In addition, the age of close-ringed birds is guaranteed. Closed rings are put on the birds' feet between the sixth and tenth day of life. They are the bird's identity card, giving its date of birth, the emblem of the breeding society, the breeder's number, and the number of the bird itself.

The most popular purchase for the home is male songsters. Anyone who wishes to enjoy the song of two such birds should position the cages in such a way that the birds can hear but not see each other. Many people decide to place the two cages one on top of the other, thus encouraging an acoustic competition. If the birds receive a normal diet it cannot be regarded as cruelty to leave the cages in that position. One cage (referring to indoor cages for canaries) must never accommodate more than one male. On no account must the hobbyist try his luck with even just two males. Such experiments invariably result in fierce fighting.

Apart from being supplied with food, the newly purchased canary should be left in perfect peace for a few days so that it has a chance to get used to its new, strange surroundings. Normally very few days elapse before the bird starts to sing.

The pleasure and excitement experienced by the keeper are incomparably greater if he acquires a pair of canaries and sets up a breeding cage for them. To watch the family life of these charming little creatures in his own home is a fascinating, rewarding experience for the naturalist. And what he has to give in return, in the way of time and money, is so very little. When there are children in the house bird-breeding in the home is of considerable educational value as well.

Anyone who has become a genuine "bird host," heart and soul, will want to have a go at breeding birds some day. There is a tremendous difference between simply buying birds in order to look after them for the rest of their lives and actually being able to do one's bit for the continuation of the species to which one's pets belong.

The price to be paid for a female canary, where the song varieties are concerned, is much lower than that for a male. When we buy color birds the difference in price is much slighter. As for the form or posture varieties, there is no difference at all. If anything, an individual female is more expensive than a male. However, as is the case with all pure-bred animals, prices vary considerably. Beginners are often baffled and confused by this, and no wonder. There is absolutely no reason why prices should not be uniform. If the birds are in the same good condition as regards plumage and health, there is no difference between individual animals and no cause for different pricing.

Domestic animals bred for very specific racial characteristics are another matter. Here we do get differences; no bird is identical to the other. One bird is less "characteristic" while the other comes much closer to the ideal of its particular breed. In the older branches of domestic animal breeding (where horses, dogs, pigeons, or rabbits are concerned for example) everyone knows that purebred champions are of much greater value than poor specimens that barely deserve the breed's name. Many breeders' associations protect themselves against possible cross-breeding by means of a centrally kept breeding record—a conscientious account of the animals' origins. Canary breeding has not yet advanced to that stage. The sole stumbling block appears to be the technical execution which is somewhat complex and, above all, costly. Years ago, in Munich, a breeders' society for color and type canaries already kept a central breeding record and achieved the very best of results with it. The German master of color-canary breeding, Julius Henninger, had already made up a system using a "proof-of-origin card" for color canaries, which unfortunately has fallen into oblivion. However, because of the ever-increasing number of new colors in canary breeding, this system will probably come into its own one day. The certificate of origin is an excellent aid to line breeding, although it must of course be kept discriminatingly, conscientiously, and above all honestly, if it is to serve its purpose.

In the meantime the closed leg band that the *Deutsche Kanarienzuchter-Bund* (German canary-breeders' association) distributes annually among its members remains the only document of pure breeding we have where the canary is concerned.

GREENFOOD FOR CANARIES

Partly because people could not be bothered but also because many canary owners live in unfavorable surroundings, it has virtually been forgotten that seeding wild plants constitute an excellent food for canaries. Old books on canaries repeatedly draw attention to certain food plants which are of great value in bird nutrition. Thanks to all

1

1 and **2.** Curling or frilling of feathers occurs most extensively in the Parisian frilled canary. Vogelpark Walsrode photos.
3. A Dutch frilled canary is slightly smaller and not as frilly or curly as a Parisian. A Vogelpark Walsrode photo.
4. The appearance of the humpbacked Italian frilled canary is unique; it is slender-boned, high-shouldered and with unfeathered thighs. A Vogelpark Walsrode photo.

those vitamin supplements in liquid or powder form the knowledge of this natural and cheap hoard of first-rate delicacies has almost been lost.

Bird lovers are people who delight in nature as a whole and take pleasure in going for walks in the fresh air. Why not, then, return from these relaxing walks with a beautiful gift for canaries in the form of a small bunch of weeds? Pinned to the bars of the cage with a clothes pin, they are not just a nutritious dietary supplement rich in vitamins but also give our pets something interesting to do. Just how thorough and expert the birds are at picking out the seeds has to be seen to be believed. It is quite amazing how skillfully they can employ the beak, that perfect tool nature has designed for them.

When collecting plants, however, we must always make sure that the area concerned has not been sprayed with chemicals of any kind. Many local authorities believe in routine spraying. If in doubt, therefore, it is advisable to check with them. Unsuitable, too, as regards the collecting of food plants, are the edges of paths much frequented by dogs, for obvious reasons. People with a garden do not have these problems, they can find all the plants they want in their own territory. For the rest, it might be an idea to ask the owner of a garden for permission to pick a bunch of weeds on their land from time to time.

Now let me introduce the most important of the food plants. All of these are very common and can be found practically everywhere.

Chickweed is a species of stitchwort that is probably the best known food plant of all. It is plentiful from early spring to late fall. With a bit of experience one can even track it down during the winter months. Chickweed does particularly well on soil treated with manure from farm animals. Anyone who is unable to locate chickweed in his area should look for it at his nearest nursery. There it is a constant companion of cultivated plants, both in the greenhouse and out in the open air. The whole plant is eaten, stalks, leaves and seeds. Chickweed is best harvested with its roots, then it will keep fresh longer. If broken off, the plant wilts rapidly, although it will recover when placed in a jar of water. Transplanted into a flower pot, chickweed keeps for a long time and can be harvested again and again. The plant requires a lot of nourishment and plenty of water.

Dandelion is so widely known that I need not introduce it. Canaries are very partial to dandelion leaves, and many breeders regard this food plant as the most important one of all. The first seeds start to ripen at the end of April, and from May to June they become the main rearing-food for free-living finches too, especially bullfinch, greenfinch, and goldfinch. Wherever possible, canary breeders should take the trouble to collect immature dandelion seeds. They will be astonished to find that the usual rearing-food with toast and hard-boiled egg or the commercial rearing-mixture is left uneaten. All my type canaries certainly display a preference for this natural rearing-food and seem to enjoy feeding it to their chicks, although these varieties are normally not very keen on doing their parental duties.

Birds fed in outdoor aviaries can be given the whole plant including the stem. The plant is at its best when the petals have turned brownish and are dropping off but the seeds are not yet exposed. Those keeping their birds indoors, in the home, would do well to cut off the "parachute" of fine hair (the pappus) that grows above the seed. Stored in plastic bags in the freezer compartment of the refrigerator, this valuable food will keep for up to two weeks. There have even been successful experiments to keep immature dandelion seeds in the deep-freeze for months. These methods of preservation can only be welcomed, particularly by the breeder of exotic birds, whose pets have to raise their young at a time of year when nothing green is growing outside and no fresh, milky seeding plants can be found.

Groundsel has long been known as a food plant for canaries. Groundsel is common in gardens, fields, and on rubbish heaps. By April the seeds are usually advanced enough for the plant to be harvested. It is a greenfood canaries are always interested in, except when chickweed is given at the same time.

Coltsfoot, one of the earliest flowering plants in spring, is another member of our native flora that is ready for eating and at its best as early as April. The pappus of this plant is less easy to remove, which makes coltsfoot somewhat more difficult to collect.

Both *ribwort plantain* and *greater plantain* have been used as food plants for canaries from the earliest times. In some German cities it is actually possible to purchase these plants in small bunches ready for use. Greater plantain is marginally the better of the two varieties; its anthers extend further down, too. Placed in a jar of water, greater plantain will keep fresh for a few days. The plant should not be collected until the capsules start to turn brown. This is when the right degree of ripeness has been reached. Before that the seeds are still green and too soft. Ribwort plantain tends to be less popular with the birds, particularly when other seed varieties are available as well.

Knotgrass, which, however, does not appear until late in the year (usually not before the middle of August), is popular with all finches. The other varieties of knotgrasses may be collected, too, although they are fairly tough plants. The best way to deal with them is simply to cut off the seed-bearing shoots.

Sow-thistle, a compositae like groundsel and dandelion, is another

1. A variegated recessive white canary. Photo by H.V. Lacey.
2. Randomly variegated specimens are not desired by many fanciers. 3. The serin resembles the wild canary, although it is a smaller, more compact and more colorful bird. Serins adapt well and live long in captivity. A Vogelpark Walsrode photo.

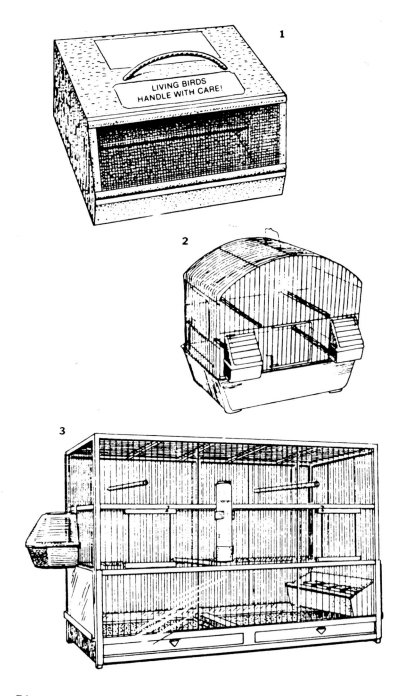

LIVING BIRDS
HANDLE WITH CARE!

fairly common plant that grows as a weed in open spaces, on paths, and in fields. It can be collected from June onwards and is sometimes around until well into November. Like all compositaes, this one too may be picked whenever it is available. It does not matter how mature or otherwise its seeds are.

Cornflower belongs to the same plant family. While it cannot be said to be one of the canary's favorites, there is no reason why we should not include a few seed-bearing stems of this plant among our bunch of weeds.

Shepherd's purse, on the other hand, is a very popular food plant. From June onwards it is fairly common in dry spots. We pick the whole plant and place it in a jar of water until required. The birds are very fond of laboring away on the "purse" and there is no doubt that they like the flavor of the seeds.

Grasses, in canary-breeding circles, are of only limited popularity as food plants. Unjustly so, for they include very valuable and welcome varieties which breeders of exotic finches have known and made use of from the very beginning. All sorts of grasses may be included in one's bunch of weeds, but preference should be given to the annual meadow-grass. This is a small grass that grows wherever it can find a spare patch of soil. Its scientific name is *Poa annua.* The hobbyist who is not familiar with this plant should ask a botanist to help him identify it.

The above is a brief description of the most important food plants. I have confined my rough selection to those plants that are most common and best known. That are are many more species which are suitable as canary food goes without saying.

1. Canaries are transported in this type of crate. Food and water must be present throughout the trip. 2. A canary cage suited for the living room. It is 40 cm long, with a plastic bottom and external feeding troughs. 3. A flight cage with attached bath. It can also be used for breeding.

1. The Scotch fancy is now a rarity, but this posture is still being perfected by a few dedicated breeders. Photo by H.V. Lacey. 2. Frosting of the feathers results when feathers are not pigmented throughout. A Vogelpark Walsrode photo.

Left: An engraved cup is just one of the many kinds of awards (ribbons, plaques, plates, certificates, etc.) that a canary show winner may receive. Photo by H. V. Lacey. *Below:* View of a border canary show in England. Uniform stock cages are seen on the right, while the show cages are neatly arranged on the left. Photo by L. E. Perkins.

Song and Beauty Contests

In accordance with specific concepts of their breeders, all our domestic animals are divided into breeds or varieties, and each of these has a particular purpose assigned to it. Where the canary, the budgerigar, and other small birds are concerned, this purpose is solely that they are suitable as companions in the home. The five centuries of the canary's domestic history, during which 500 generations of birds of this species were born into human care, have resulted in a multitude of deviations from the original bird from the Canary Islands. Measured in terms of a human life, this period of time spanned by 500 generations comes to about 15,000 years. This is what one has to keep in mind when comparing the different varieties with each other. The other

1. Crested Glosters are usually called Gloster coronas. There is an imperfection in the corona of this yellow Gloster— black should not extend to the back of the neck. A Vogelpark Walsrode photo. **2.** A crested red factor canary. **3.** The crest is also found in individuals of the Lancashire breed called "coppies." Crestless individuals are called "plainheads." Photo by H.V. Lacey.

2

3 →

aspect of the canary's history—how it came to be a domestic animal—is related in earlier chapters. Here I intend to introduce the bird lover to the canary fancy, pursued as a hobby by many thousands of breeders.

In Germany alone there are about 20,000 people who devote their leisure time to the "sport" of competitive canary breeding. The sole purpose of the contests is to measure the birds of the individual breeders against the standard for an "ideal" canary.

For the song varieties these are song contests which take place annually in November and December. The birds are trained by highly specific methods in special song cages for these events, and are expected to perform their repertoire in front of the judges within 30 minutes. At smaller shows there is only a single judge, whereas at the bigger contests the points are awarded by a panel of three judges. The reason for this lies in the division of the scale of points into three parts. The maximum that can be awarded for the best performance is 90 points. The birds are submitted in groups of four. All four must bear the same breeder's number, as proof that they come from the same breeding stock.

The canary fancier who is hoping for the highest distinction can only achieve this with young birds of the current year. In fact, older males are banned from the more important contests. Only the smaller, local shows allow them to be entered.

The winners of the local contests meet at regional level and compete against each other. However, to be allowed to take part here, they need to have accumulated a certain minimum number of points. Those who emerge first and second in any particular region are permitted to compete for the title at the national level. This is the general rule governing entry for the annual song contests.

The regulations for exhibitions that concern the breeders of color and type canaries, as well as for those of canaries crossed with other finches, are of course different. Here we have "beauty contests," where birds taking part are judged purely for their appearance. A detailed assessment card is drawn up with the individual positions of their racial characteristics. All sorts of color canaries, for example, are judged by means of a scale divided into seven sections. These, in the same sequence as the one I am using here, are as follows:

(1) Basic color up to 30 points; this refers to the carotenoid pigment (lipochrome) of the bird.
(2) Dark color, including markings (melanins), up to 20 points.
(3) Feather quality up to 15 points.
(4) Size (ideal size = 14 cm) up to 10 points.
(5) Conformation up to 10 points.
(6) Condition and carriage up to 10 points.

(7) General effect up to 5 points. Groups of four of the same color stock, which have been entered for the highest award at the national level, may earn up to 6 points extra for uniformity.

Rigid compliance to guiding principles, together with an exactly defined ideal which is known as the "Standard," help to guarantee an objective and uniform assessment at all exhibitions.

The breeding of color canaries only started to enjoy a wider popularity about 1955. The range of colors has, of course, increased tremendously since the canary was crossed with the hooded siskin, *Spinus cucullatus*, from Venezuela. All our reddish canaries are, in fact, derived from a hereditary character of this red and black siskin.

While the song canaries require a proper training, (which was described in detail in the chapter on canary song), exhibition birds need no more than a brief period of acclimatization prior to the show to help them get used to the new cage. This is to ensure that they are not shy or fluttering about in a wild panic when coming before the panel of judges. In the event of the latter, they would lose points in the "carriage" category.

Some type varieties, whose main characteristic is a certain abnormal stance (usually sharp upright, not looking like a finch at all), require a longer training period.

The most important time of the year for the color breeder who wants to exhibit his birds is the molting period. The color is only deposited in the appropriate feather cells while the feather remains enclosed within the sheath. This applies both to the melanin (dark feather pigment) produced by the body itself (without "raw materials") and to the basic, or ground, color, which is a lipochrome or carotenoid (named after the pigment found in the carrot). These yellow-to-red pigments are widely distributed in nature. The canary has to take them into the body, in the form of raw materials, with the food; only then can the lipochrome be manufactured. The way carotenoids act on canary feathers is now very well known. The breeders strive very hard, by careful planning of the birds' diet, to achieve the brightest possible red in the basic color of their red-factor canaries. Ever since synthetic canthaxanthin (which corresponds to the red feather color of the hooded siskin), has become available, heated arguments have been going on about the exact definition of a natural diet with respect to color birds. Fed to red-factor canaries in pure form, canthaxantin leads to an exaggeration of the red feather color (often as far as violet). The bird is genetically quite unequipped to manufacture such a color from raw materials it has taken in with the food. Viewed thus, the feeding of canthaxanthin equals artificial coloring, which is of course strictly prohibited. However, many

1. A red-factor bird, if fed color foods at molting time, will show a much redder plumage after the molt. This intense color is not permanent and will be lost in the subsequent molt, unless the bird is color-fed again. Photo by H.V. Lacey. 2. A silver agate opal. Canaries with such reduced pigmentation are sometimes called "dilutes." A Vogelpark Walsrode photo.

green plants (notably immature seeding plants) contain carotenoids. The color that is finally assumed by the young birds in the fall is the one great concern of all color breeders. They all do their best, and each keeps his secret as to how he achieves an optimal molt for his color birds.

Not infrequently one hears from one canary keeper or another that his birds had changed color after the molt. On a biological basis alone this is an impossibility. Nevertheless, if there is a change in appearance, then the cause is invariably an external one. The first thing to look for is dirt. Dust could be adhering to the feathers, giving them a matt-like appearance, or the change could simply be due to mechanical wear and tear of the feathers' edges, which could result in an altered shade. This phenomenon is not uncommon in the bird world, and among the finch family specifically the chaffinch and linnet are good examples. Here, nature has provided this protective arrangement: in the fall, after their completed molt, the two species are not nearly as brightly colored as in the spring. The brighter spring colors are not the result of another molt, however. What happens is that the edges of the small feathers wear away and the pigments that were deposited during the late summer become visible. Carotenoids deposited in the birds' feathers are so stable that they keep for years, without altering, even in a stuffed specimen, as a visit to any museum of natural history will show.

Exhibiting as a "sport" originated in England, the classic country of animal breeding. Today as ever, the National Exhibition continues to be the greatest bird show in the world, although it is confined to British canary varieties only. While in Central Europe the birds are judged according to a scale of points, birds in England compete for the best places in several different classes and always as individuals. Obviously the birds are always judged against an ideal of whatever variety they belong to, but no points are awarded. The first seven birds, the winners from each class receive a certificate. A breeder who has managed to win certificates for his show birds in the individual classes rightly feels pleased with himself. The best birds of each class then compete for "best birds" of their variety. Somewhere between these two events the best birds of each sex are selected, as males and females are exhibited in separate classes.

Thus, the English method of judging is a constant comparison of the birds that have been entered, until at last the "best bird of all classes" becomes the winner of the show. All this takes place in a single day. The many thousands of birds on exhibit (record number of entries nearly 10,000 birds) can be rapidly evaluated by this method. This has the advantage that the show birds are only away from home for a very limited period. A mammoth show in England like the one just described lasts only from Wednesday to the following Sunday. A German show at the national level, on the other hand, spans a period of 12 days or more, which means the birds are away for 14 days. This technical problem appears to be of considerable significance in the future development of canary exhibiting. The strain on the birds is immense when they are away from home and on show for so long.

The breeders, as well as those responsible for organizing these shows, must make sure that the birds taking part will still be fit for breeding the following spring. Canary shows in Germany are held for a minimum of 100 birds. This applies to the smaller clubs as well. The larger societies and county clubs today already exhibit up to 500 canaries. At the national show in 1968-9, around 1,000 birds of the various exhibition varieties had been entered. When we look at these figures, which are so very much lower than the British ones, we have to bear in mind that in Germany a preliminary selection takes place. Entrants for the national show must first qualify for this privilege by doing well in shows at the regional and local levels.

The country where the canary is most popular—if breeding statistics are anything to go by—is Holland. This small country boasts of 35,000 organized breeders, and roughly a million leg bands are distributed each year.

Since World War II the exhibiting of canaries has undergone a tremendous development from an international point of view. The *Confederation Ornithologique Mondiale* (C.O.M.) has organized associations in over 30 countries all over the world. Every year two international shows are held: in Western Europe for participants from the northern hemisphere and in Latin America for the southern half of the globe. The main tasks of these organizations, all of which are run purely for and by hobbyists, are to set up guide lines for assessment, a uniform nomenclature of varieties and colors, and reliable genetic tables with symbols that can be internationally understood. The contact with professional ornithologists working in a scientific capacity ensures a sound professional foundation without which a hobbyist organization of this dimension could not hope to function. The hobbyist literature which started off somewhat amateurish and over-sentimental has long since grown into a proper canary science worthy of serious attention.

In recent years, scientific symposia on the canary have already been held at which the genetics, development of races, and relationships within the sub-family of true finches (*Carduelinae*) were discussed. The results of such scientific conferences quickly extend their influence to the work of the breeding societies, and most particularly where the im-

1 and **2.** Parent canaries regurgitate soft food directly into the chick's mouth. Rearing food is available commercially, but many breeders make their own formula from certain basic ingredients (eggs, soaked seeds, bread, baby cereals, honey, sugar, etc.). Photo 1 by H.V. Lacey, photo 2 by Vogelpark Walsrode. **3.** These chicks are only a few days old. In a couple more weeks they will be able to feed themselves and hop about. Photo by H.V. Lacey.

← **1**

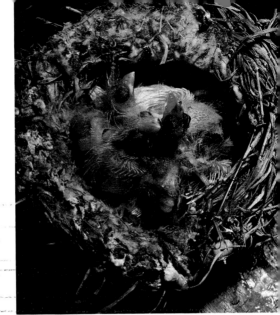

3

2

portant new mutations of the color canaries and the color combinations they make possible are concerned.

An international color table which is actually in use is a kind of "world currency" of color-canary breeding. With this system the language spoken by the breeder or hobbyist is immaterial; by using the international symbols he can express any color as a short formula. As yet there is no other breeders' organization (if we disregard the commercially oriented producers of domestic cattle, etc.) that can boast a similar arrangement. The greater the number of countries in which color breeding gains a footing, the more its importance will grow. Let us hope that all breeders concerned will make a point of using the international table.

When we further consider that the standards used by the judges in all 30 countries are identical, we really begin to understand the wide-ranging importance of an institution such as that represented by the COM.

It must be stressed that the COM has done its share toward educating people about the importance of international nature-conservation and, is also maintaining contact with the World Wildlife Fund (W.W.F.). Today, as the natural ranges of free-living animals are being increasingly restricted and destroyed, certain species of birds can no longer be freely collected in order to be sold as pets. Unfortunately, some people are still holding on to the picture-book fantasy that tropical countries continue to be inexhaustible reservoirs of exotic birds. In fact, many countries have already imposed a general ban on exports. The understanding of all bird lovers is vital here. They must see that uncontrolled collecting may, if nothing else, banish certain species from their natural range. Other endangered animals are now receiving the attention of the zoo directors in their international association. Organizations of bird breeders can make a valuable contribution toward worldwide bird protection by informing their members which species are endangered and no longer offering them for unrestricted sale. Over and above that, breeders could form special associations with the aim of devoting themselves to the conservation of certain species of birds. One such breeders' society already in existence is concerned with the conservation of Australian finches for which, of course, a ban on exports was imposed by the Australian government nearly ten years ago.

Every bird lover should contribute something, however little, towards the conservation of the animal world. More likely than not, his native town will give him an opportunity to be of help. It is not the obligatory nesting box behind the house or the birdfeeder in winter in the front garden that makes all the difference. What is really vital is that such relatively unspoiled habitats of native animals and plants that still exist are taken into consideration and, if at all possible, allowed to remain by our town planners. Sometimes the vigilance and prompt, appropriate action of bird lovers can work this miracle. In some cases, for example, a petition with many signatures may succeed in persuading the pertinent authorities to carry out protective measures.

Thinking and caring about matters like these must surely be expected from anyone who considers himself a bird lover in the true sense of the word. I trust the readers of this volume about the canary will go along with me on this. Everything in our world is subject to perpetual change. Like the evolution of canary breeding itself, the attitude toward it and the motives for it have changed too. Nobody today buys a canary because he feels a need for background music. This much is certain, however: no one can hope to become a proper bird-keeper, let alone a proper breeder, unless he is deeply interested in and absolutely devoted to this hobby.

New-color roller canaries. Crossing rollers with other breeds is not common practice, however. Photo by H.V. Lacey.